COLLEGE KNOWLEDGE BOOK

Get Up. Gear Up. Move Up.

A Resource For Educational Success

Ernesto Mejia & Carlos Ojeda Jr.

D1472342

CoolSpeak Publishing Company

Book design and cover design by Carlos Ojeda Jr.

ISBN-13: **978-0615765969**

Table of Contents

Introduction

You're in high school right now. Maybe you're in tenth grade, looking at eleventh in a few months and the last thing on your mind is college. That's okay.

For now.

What happens in another year when the decisions you need to make about college come at you with lightning speed?

Perhaps you don't even think that you can get into college. Maybe school thing isn't your thing. Hey, when we're young, we truly do believe the world is there for the taking, that we can do anything we want and we'll still be tough and cool and hip.

Let me tell you something, though. People with college degrees earn a lot more money that those with just high school diplomas. With a college degree, you get many more opportunities to find the career that you *want*, not just the one that you can get when you're out of options.

This book is designed to help you understand the true value of a college education and that you can truly enroll in college, make your dreams come true, and live the life you want to.

Don't let whatever may have happened in the past discourage you. Don't let a teacher who told you that you'll never amount to anything get inside your head. Life is short. Before you know it, you're going to be thirty looking back on these years with a much different perspective. Ask around. Go find a few thirty-something people in your neighborhood and ask them what they thought when they were your age and what they know now. You might be surprised at what you hear.

College is a gateway. It doesn't guarantee you anything, but it opens the door to so many other possibilities in life and when you take the chance, when you make the commitment to go to college and you work hard and earn your degree, you will have a much broader view of the world and the world around you. You will be able to truly see all of the possibilities that exist out there for you.

This book is designed to give you a foundation, a blueprint, if you will, to get in gear, to start thinking about college and to begin to take the steps *now* that will help you prepare for that moment when you're ready to put your applications together and send them off to different universities and colleges.

No matter what grade you're in now, it's never too early or late to Get in Gear. So what are you waiting for? Let's get this thing in gear.

Why College is Important

You've probably heard your teachers and maybe even your parents tell you this over and over: *college is important.*

Yeah, but why?

That's what you want to know about, isn't it? Why is college so important? Perhaps you've paid attention to the news lately and how so many recent college graduates are out of work, can't find work, and are still living at home with their mother and father.

The cost of tuition keeps going up and that seems to keep the dream of a college education out of reach for more people every year. So why would you want to think about it now, given that more than 25% of all recent college grads still can't find work?

The first point to make here is that those figures can be deceiving. If 1 out of every 4 college graduates can't find work, then we have to explore the 'why'. 25% sounds like a lot, but in reality, you have to understand that there are many different degrees to choose from, many disciplines that you can study. You could earn an engineering job, a psychology degree, or a law degree, just to name three off the top of my head.

Many kids go into college without the slightest clue about what they want to do with their life. The *average college student changes their major 3 (three) times during their college career*.[i] That's significant. That's about finding your way, finding your motivation. Still, it's also a sign that many college students don't actually figure out what they want to do until after they graduate, so they end up with a 'liberal arts' degree, or other generic degree.

Those degrees don't add much value to your resume when you're looking for work. Therefore, even with a college degree in hand, if it's a basic degree you'll still find it difficult to obtain a good job when you graduate.

But think about this: a college graduate (with a bachelor's degree) earns, on average, $26,000 *a year* more than a person with just a high school diploma. That's just on average. And that's every single year.

During the course of your life, if you settle for a high school diploma and decide to skip college, you'll earn about $1.3 million dollars. That sounds like a lot, but divide that by 40 working years (and most likely more) and you'll find that it's actually $30,000 a year. That's about average.

Now, a person with a bachelor's degree will earn, on average $2.3 million. With a master's degree, they will earn $2.6 million, and with a doctorate degree, they'll earn $3.3 million.[ii]

So if money is what catches your interest, how do those figures look? Almost a million dollars more during a lifetime with a college education as opposed to only a high school diploma.

Experience

Let's set the money factor aside for a moment, though.

Going to college will offer you a wide breadth of experiences. You'll be able to take a wide range of classes that will give you a glimpse into what it might be like to work in a specific field.

Has astronomy intrigued you? You might want to become an astrophysicist.

Do you enjoy building things? How about engineering?

Maybe you enjoy rearranging your room every so often, getting the most space out of what you have. You might be interested in interior design.

Perhaps you love working with computers. Information technology could be your preference.

Do you find that you're good at helping friends deal with tough circumstances? Then you might pursue a degree in psychology.

In college, you will have the opportunity to gain a greater understanding of a variety of different fields. You'll be able to sample them and find which one fits not only your personality, but your passion.

When you have a passion for the work you do, not only will it seem less like work and more like fun, but you'll be more apt to excel at it. When you enjoy what you do for a living, it affects everything else in your life in a positive way. From relationships to community outreach, from hobbies to friends, your entire life becomes a much different landscape of opportunity.

People who go off to college often report that they're lives become much different in the long run. While you could go to a local college and live at home, there's something to be said for living on campus.

You learn the value of responsibility. You make new friends who share your interests. You see a completely different world than the one you grew up surrounded by. You quickly realize that there are so many other possibilities that exist in the world that you will begin to feel inspired.

Life is about experiences and if you decide not to go to college, if you think that it's just not right for you, that may be fine. But you will miss out on experiences that would and will change your life, for the most part for the better.

The more you expose yourself to things that are different, that are outside the normal mode of operation for you, the more you will change as an individual.

The average individual who decided that a high school degree was plenty for them will still be living at home, usually in the basement or a converted garage room of their parents' house when they're 25. Almost 30% may still be living at home when they turn 30. The average college graduate will be on his or her own by the time they're 23.

What kind of experience do you want to have?

This question is about lifestyle. What do you want to be when you're 25? Do you want to be married with children, living in a decent house in a good neighborhood? Do you want to have good friends with whom you can get together on a regular basis? Do you want to be able to travel and take a vacation every year?

Consider this: If you'll earn, on average $30,000 a year at most with a high school diploma, you'll take home about $26,000 of that after taxes. If you pay $700 a month in rent for a small one-bedroom apartment, then utilities such as electric and heat and water, that will leave you with about $14,000 a year. If you own a car, then you have to fill it with gas to get back and forth to your job, and insure it, so you're talking about another $300 to $400 a month. Food will cost you maybe $200 a month. And these numbers are only for you living alone, with no girlfriend or boyfriend. This leaves you with less than $8,000 a year for other expenses, and there will be plenty. That will leave you about $150 a week for clothing, games, movies, eating out, and anything else you may want.

Is that the kind of life you'll be content to lead? If so, then that's fine. Grab your high school diploma and go pursue it. Just remember, that $30,000 figure is an average. You might actually earn a lot less during the first 10 or 20 years of working.

If you want more out of life, then think about college.

Today, more companies are requiring at least a college degree, at a minimum, before they will even consider hiring you. Go to your local pharmacy and you can apply for a job ringing at a register. You'll get paid minimum wage and that's fine for a high school student. But ask them what you'd need to apply to be an assistant manager. You might be surprised.

Every year, more of these companies are demanding that their management have at least earned a college degree.

And right now there are jobs that haven't even been created yet that will require you to have a college degree. Sports medicine, physical therapy, web development, and much more all require college degrees. Video game programming and even testing (yes, you can get paid to play video games) all require college degrees now.

A college degree will open up so many doors and possibilities for you that a high school diploma can't provide.

That, in itself, is one of the most compelling reasons to pursue a college education.

When you're young, you have the world at your feet. You have an endless stream of possibilities open before you. Each choice you make either keeps them open or closes them one at a time.

When you head off to college, you keep most of them open. If you don't, the doors close and that limits what you'll be able to accomplish in your life.

You may not know what you want to do yet, but in time you will know. Get in gear and make college a plan for your life.

1. On average how much money will a person with a Bachelor's degree earn over a lifetime?

2. At what age is a college graduate independent and living on their own?

3. If you only have a high school diploma how much money will you really have left to spend a year after paying all living expenses?

What Colleges Want

"I don't have the grades for college."

That's a common excuse why many kids avoid the topic of college. In reality, though, colleges look for much more than just the grades you produced in high school.

The truth is that if you really want to pursue a college degree, then you can make it happen. The first step is to understand what colleges want and what they're looking for in their future students. *KnowHow2Go* provides some great information to help you plan ahead: http://www.knowhow2go.org.

Grades

The most notable thing that we all consider when applying for college is our grades. While this is important, having a 'C' average isn't going to keep you from achieving the education that you want.

Of course, you're not going to get into Harvard, Yale, or MIT with a 'C' average, and you'll limit the type of universities and colleges that you can apply for, but average grades will get you in the door at any number of institutions for higher education, as they're referred to.

Depending on where you are in your high school career, you may have a lot of time to bring your grades up. However, even if you're in the latter part of the eleventh grade, for example, or even a senior, whatever you've earned will be what the colleges you apply to see.

So let's say you have a C- average. What are your options? Is college out of the question? Not at all.

Focus first on junior colleges. Enroll in a few college level classes, even when you're still in high school, and work hard to get the best grades that you can.

Colleges aren't generally looking to see what you've already accomplished; they're looking to see your *potential*.

What will you be capable of when you come to their school?

You are most likely capable of far more than you give yourself credit at the moment. If you can show them that your C average isn't your full potential, you'll be more likely to convince a college or university to accept you into their program.

What Are Acceptance Rates in Colleges?

Depending on which schools you apply to, you'll find a varying degree of acceptance rates. Most junior colleges will accept you regardless of how you performed in high school, and these can give you a launching pad to turn your life around.

Acceptance rates at some of the premiere schools in the country tend to be in the single digits (8% at Brown, 7% at Princeton, 5% at Stanford University, etc.), but rates are as high as 60-65% for other universities.[iii]

If the acceptance rate is 20%, for example, That means if 100,000 students applied to the school, 20,000 would be accepted. Or, 1 out of every 5 applicants get in. If a college has an acceptance rate of 60%, that means 6 out of every 10 students who apply will be accepted, or 3 out of every 5. Some universities have even higher acceptance rates, especially junior or community colleges.

So when it comes to your grades, don't let poor ones discourage you from applying to college. If you want it, you'll get in.

Grades end up being the simple classifying tool that admissions committees use to determine whether they will look at an applicant's transcript. If their benchmark (standard that they use to determine acceptability) is 90 and above, then a 76 average is likely to earn you a quick 'Thanks, but no thanks.'

You see, colleges are run by human beings and human beings understand that there's a lot that makes up a person, and there could be issues that a student had growing up, challenges that he or she dealt with that others didn't endure, and that's why grades are only a small aspect of the decision making process.

There are a number of other factors, including any sports that you play, activities that you take part in, work history, school government, volunteer work, your passions and desires, and community involvement.

Colleges want *well-rounded* students and I have seen a number of people with perfect grades (4.0, or 100, or A+, depending on your point of view) who were denied entry into certain programs or universities because they weren't involved in anything outside of their grades.

Activities

Do you play sports? If so, that's great. If not, have you been involved in any other activity that was organized by your school or the town or city in which you live? Sports are the number one activity that we tend to think about, but there are numerous other activities that you could already have taken part in but didn't consider it important for college.

The YMCA offers a host of activities that you may take part in. If you play basketball in a league after school or on the weekends, you took part in an activity. Remember, though, that playing with your friends on the corner isn't what we're talking about here.

We're talking about organized activities that bring together different individuals who may or may not know one another and work together to accomplish a specific goal. Walking around town handing out flyers to help raise money for a new youth resource center could constitute an activity. Taking part in a marathon or other type of race would be considered an activity.

Think about what you've done, what you've been a part of since you started school. Write them all down on a sheet of paper and then evaluate each one to see whether they might show your desire to do more than just attend classes.

That's what colleges want. They want students who are going to be involved in school outside of the classroom.

Groups and Programs

Chess club, student council, or any other type of group that you've been a part of, even for a short time, can add weight to your college application. Maybe you joined a group that was trying to gain more student privileges or helped a political candidate try to win an election.

Maybe you took part in a youth empowerment program or attended a seminar on basketball, or even a clinic. These are all considered groups and programs that would look great on your application.

It's important to remember that your goal is not to throw everything into your application, but anything that is relevant and that offered you some ability to learn and grow is something that you want to include in your application.

Passion

Admissions committees (the people who make the decision about whether to admit you into the school or not) want to see passion within their prospective students. They want to see that you have a desire to have a great life and possibly even contribute in some way to society around you.

Maybe you tutor fellow students in a subject that you ace without much effort. Perhaps you love working with younger kids and volunteer some of your time to babysit or teach them skills on the ball field.

Maybe you believe that homelessness is a major problem and you volunteer at a soup kitchen every weekend handing out food.

There are so many things for us to be passionate about, but if you stand around watching life go by, then what are you going to contribute to a college in the future? Step up and get involved. Show the school of your choice that you are driven, motivated, and ready to help make theirs a better college for just being there.

Community

Throughout your community, there are a number of programs and groups and functions that you can be a part of. Being involved in your community could be something as simple as assisting in street cleanup, picking up garbage from your block, or helping to raise money for charity.

You could be part of a group of people who walk around town after the elementary schools let out, making sure that young students get home safe and without being harassed.

Reaching out to other students about bullying and trying to work toward ending bullying is a way to become involved in your community.

Community is about the people around us, the people whom we see every day.

Colleges want to see that you are going to strive to succeed, that you are going to be involved in the community where the college is located, and that you could possibly be a role model for others in the future.

They aren't actually looking for students who will just exist and get by. There are plenty of those.

They want exceptional *people* and your grades are only a small part of the larger picture. Your grades don't really define you; your actions and entire life, in *and* out of school are what define you.

Show the colleges that you would like to attend that you are driven, dedicated, and determined.

Why not stay on top of what *current* college students are talking about and doing? You can with a number of colleges across the country through CollegeWeeklyLive.com: http://www.collegeweeklylive.com.

Completion Rates

Colleges have plenty of students start out their educations, but never finish them. In fact, according to a Harvard University study, just 56% of students who start their 4-year degree programs finish within 6 years.[iv]

That's *just slightly more than ½ of all college freshman earn their degrees*. Of course, that doesn't count those individuals who eventually go back to finish beyond the six year mark.

So why don't more freshmen end up completing their degrees?

Because most students unfortunately don't really know what they want to do, aren't ready for college, and don't think beyond the narrow window of what they experienced in high school.

You can stand out. You can be different. You can show the college of your choice that you mean business and you're ready to be an exceptional part of their school system.

How do you show them this?

By setting yourself up for success now.

1. What website provides some great information to help you plan ahead and show you what colleges want?

2. Besides looking for what you've already accomplished what else are colleges looking for in potential students?

3. What is the acceptance rate at some of the premier colleges in the USA?

Setting Yourself Up For Success

Success doesn't just happen. It doesn't fall into your lap while you're sitting around playing video games all day or hanging out with your friends after school.

Success is something that runs away from you and if you're not willing to catch up to it, it's going to keep running away.

Every little thing that you do (and usually you'll think it's little, but they end up being big things in the end) converges and becomes something larger in the end.

Think of it like coins in a fountain. Kids love to toss pennies and nickels and dimes and quarters into a fountain and make wishes. When one person tosses a penny in, it's no big deal.

When a thousand coins are tossed in there, all you see is money.

Each step that you take is another coin in the fountain of your life. It may seem small and insignificant at the time, but it will become part of something bigger before too long. A quote attributed to Benjamin Franklin said, 'A penny saved is a penny earned.'

Today, a penny is hardly worth much at all. You probably see pennies on the ground here and there and just ignore them. Most of us do.

What about dollar bills? Would you pass those by? Most likely you'd bend down and snatch it up in your fist, and then tuck it in your pocket.

What if you found a hundred of those over two years and had saved every single one? Then you'd have a nice amount of money that you could do anything you wanted with it.

Now, each thing that you can do now toward your future may not seem like a lot, and you'll probably enjoy doing many of them, but over time they will build up and when you're ready to apply for and go off to college, you will have a nice chunk of change (emotional change) to go there with in hand.

So, what is one of the first things you should do to set yourself up for success?

Schedule the right classes.

Your Schedule

You may not enjoy English, Language Arts, or whatever they call it in your school, but it's a necessity. Most high diplomas require four years of English, Social Sciences, and Math. Yuk, right?

What about other classes? Are there subjects that interest you? Things that you want to try out and see if they're a good fit for you?

Perhaps your school offers chemistry or physics and you have an aptitude toward sciences and believe that you could do well in them. What about computer sciences? Wood shop (engineering)?

Add classes that go beyond the ordinary, that highlight your interests and will offer you a great advantage when it comes to your grades.

Be careful not to schedule too many classes, though. You can run the risk of overloading your schedule and end up struggling to get your homework done for all of your classes.

Learn to find the right balance that works for you.

The more classes you take, the more opportunities you have to bring your grades up and impress the admissions committees of these colleges and universities. Try to arrange a study hall or two in between these classes so that you'll have time to work on homework or study for an upcoming exam.

If you're taking general classes (as opposed to advanced or AP –Advanced Placement, which can count as college credit classes), and your grades are good enough to warrant moving up, then take advantage of that with one or two. When you're in advanced English or Math, for example, it adds weight to your overall grade.

For example, a student who earns an 85 average with all regular classes isn't the same as an 85 for a student who took all advanced classes. In fact, after weighting the advanced levels, that 85 could end up being an 89 or even a 90 (to the college admission's committee).

However, perhaps you worry that you won't be able to handle the workload, so you decide to schedule fewer classes in order to give yourself time to study and get everything done. This is under-scheduling and that can count against you.

Remember, http://www.knowhow2go.org is a powerful resource!

The Risk of Under-scheduling

There is a temptation among students who aim to improve their grades to schedule the bare minimum number of classes, or to avoid anything challenging. The risk in this is that the admissions committee at the college you apply to will look to see what classes you took, whether you applied yourself, and what you are capable of accomplishing.

If you take the minimum, then maybe that's all you want. Maybe that's all you're capable of doing.

So what if you earned a 93 average with your light schedule? To the college admissions committee, you didn't try very hard. You weren't really tested. What they're going to consider is that you don't have what it takes to survive at the college level.

If ½ of college freshmen fail to finish their schooling, and every college is looking for students that will not only finish, but who will build up the credibility and community of the campus, then why would they take a chance on someone who barely applies himself or herself?

They won't.

Keep a solid schedule and push yourself. An 85 average with a solid schedule will carry much more weight than a 93 with a light schedule.

How Important Are Extracurricular Activities?

As mentioned in Chapter 2, what you do outside of the classroom is going to be extremely important. Your grades get their attention, but it's your extracurricular activities that sell you.

If you're not interested in sports, that's not a problem. Sign up for a computer club, chess club, student council, or get involved in your community.

Volunteer to work at fundraisers, go to shelters in your community and see what you may be able to do in order to help out.

Below is a list of possible extracurricular activities that you can take part in:

- **Arts** – Anything artistic and creative is a great outlet for many young people. Do you like music? Are you part of the band? What about theater? Does your school have a theater production? If not, there are some throughout most towns and cities. Other arts include creative writing, photography, dance, and painting.

- **Church Activity** – There are many different youth programs in a host of churches that you can become involved in, and they are non-denominational, which means that you don't have to believe in the church's beliefs or teachings to take part in them. A number of churches are also often involved with fundraising and volunteer work helping the poor or disadvantaged in a number of communities.

- **Clubs** – Debate groups, the chess club, role playing, language clubs, skateboarding, diversity discussion groups, and more.

- **Community Activities** – Get involved in assisting at festivals, community theater, event organizing, or anything that strikes your interest.

- **Government** – Student council, prom committees, community youth boards, advisory boards, and so on.

- **Hobbies** – Most of us have hobbies of some form or another. There are generally local groups of adults and kids who share your enthusiasm for a hobby. Get involved.

- **Media** – Local radio and television networks often use youths to run errands, intern, and learn the trade. You may even be able to work on a local television production, which might lead to work on a movie set.

- **Military** – Junior ROTC and drill teams offer a great chance to stand out on a college application.

- **Music** – Band, chorus, local musical groups, through the community or church, any of these can be a great opportunity to build up your resume of extracurricular activities.

- **Sports** – School or community league teams can be a great benefit for your application process.
- **Volunteer work** – In every city and community, there are literally dozens of groups that accept volunteer work. While you won't earn any money for your time, these can be invaluable to a college application.

When you build up your success one step at a time, by the time you turn around and look back over all that you've done and accomplished, even you'll be impressed.

It's easy to overlook all of the little things that we do in life, every day, but they add up and make a difference. It will make a difference when you apply for college, too.

Need help thinking about what to get involved in? Try DoSomething.org. This resource can help you find worthy causes that will look great on a resume! http://www.dosomething.org.

Chapter 4 Get In Gear Questions

1. What is one of the first things you should do to begin setting yourself up for success?

2. What are 4 possible extra curricular activities you could do to help increase your college acceptance?

3. What site can help you find worthy causes that would look great on a resume?

How You Can Start Getting Ready

How many times have you waited until the last minute to get that assignment finished? You know, the one that your teacher assigned in the beginning of the school year but wasn't due until April.

Most of us have done this on at least one occasion. Maybe you squeaked by with the effort, maybe your grade took a hit for rushed work.

Whatever the case, when it comes to college, you don't want to wait until two days before the application deadline to start getting everything together.

Start making your plans now, no matter what grade you're in at the moment.

SAT/ACT Exams

You might have heard all about SAT or ACT exams. These are the quintessential exams of your high school career if you want to get into college. They focus on math, reading comprehension, and writing skills for the most part. These exams are essentially designed to determine how much you've actually learned throughout your school career.

For the most part, the results tend to align relatively well with the grades you've earned, but that is not always the case. There have been plenty of straight A students who scored relatively poorly on their SATs and there have been plenty of C students who aced theirs.

One of the common themes that instructors will carry through the years leading up to these exams is that you can't really study for them. In a way that's true. If you don't pay attention or understand algebra, geometry, or English, then trying to 'cram' for the test isn't going to help you much at all.

However, you can *prepare* for these tests. There are a number of programs that can provide information that will help you prepare for the tests, give you insight into what kind of questions you'll encounter, and important information that can help boost your score.

For example, when taking the SATs, when you leave an answer blank, you receive no points. However, if you fill in an answer and get it wrong, you get some points.

The more prepared you are, the better your score will end up being. If you do really well on the ACT or SAT exam, it can go a long way toward neutralizing any low grades you earn during your high school career.

Number2.com provides some great resources to help you prepare for these exams. http://www.number2.com. March2Success can also provide much needed assistance: http://www.march2success.com/index.cfm.

How Much Do These Tests Weigh on Admissions?

The question about how much these tests weight on admissions is an important one. It's also a bit abstract. For some colleges, they consider these tests decent indicators of where you are in your education, how much you've actually learned, and how well you might perform at their institution.

Some colleges rely on these tests as little more than supplementary information. A few don't even consider the scores. However, for the most part, if you do well on either of these tests (you only have to take one, though you're entitled to take both if you choose), it can outweigh some poor grades in school. On the other hand, if you earned good grades in school and do poorly on your SAT or ACT exam, this can raise questions among the admissions committee about your potential performance.

While important, the last thing you want to do is take either of these tests with a lot of stress on your mind. They aren't going to make or break your college career, hopes, or aspirations. Think of them as bonus opportunities to sell yourself to the college of your choice, then you can have a bit less stress on your mind moving forward.

Strategies to Prepare for the SAT/ACT

As mentioned, there are a number of preparatory classes and seminars that can help you prepare for the SAT or ACT exams. You will also find a number of information books in most public libraries.

The best advice is to find a book with several practice exams. Go through a few of these tests, doing the best you can, and evaluate how well you do. This will give you a foundation upon which to build.

By the time you complete three or four sample tests, you'll begin to notice a pattern: the type of math problems that are used, the type of writing or reading comprehension questions you'll face, and so on. You'll also know which ones you do well on, which ones you're comfortable with, and which ones you need to work on.

When you recognize an area that causes you trouble, seek out extra help from teachers in your school. Even if you didn't do well in their class, even if you didn't pay attention, when you show initiative and motivation to learn the material, you'll find many of them willing to assist you in some small way.

Go through the questions you got wrong and when you understand them, move on to the next. When you feel that you have a better handle on the material, take another practice exam and compare your results with your first few attempts. Continue to do this until you feel as though you're as prepared as you can be and you will go into the exam much more relaxed and confident.

What to Do in 9th, 10th, 11th, and 12th Grade to Prepare

Each year of your high school education will be important, from ninth grade through twelfth (yes, I know you figured once you got into college then you could relax a bit and let your last year go, but that's not the case).

Pay attention to the list below and you'll put yourself in a great position for applying to and then heading off to college.

For 9th grade:
- Begin to consider your course schedule for all four years. Think about your schedule from the perspective of the college admissions committee. Also, think about what might interest you as far as the type of classes you take.

- Stretch yourself. Push yourself to the edge of your abilities, if you can. When you do, you'll impress the college of your choice.

- So, you want to get straight A's and think that scheduling easy classes will do the trick. Maybe, but the colleges won't be that impressed with good grades from easy classes. They would be more impressed with average grades from tough classes.

- If you have questions (and you should) there are plenty of places and adults whom you can ask. Stop by your school guidance counselor or visit a website such as KnowHow2Go.org to take the first steps.

- Apply yourself. We're not talking about filling in applications to colleges … yet. Apply yourself to your school work. Even if you don't enjoy school, if you want the best out of life, each step you take now will make a difference in the years to come.

For 10th Grade:

- Begin to prepare for the SAT or ACT exam that you'll take in 11th grade. By preparing now, you'll give yourself plenty of time to become familiar with the types of questions and to begin reviewing or better learning the material that is covered.

- Re-evaluate your course schedule. Are you challenged? Are you exploring your interests? Finding new ones? If not, stretch yourself even more.

For 11th Grade:

- This is the year to take the SAT or ACT exams.

- Discuss with your guidance counselor which test would be ideal for you.

- Schedule the test.

- On test day, remember to remain relaxed and don't leave any question blank. Even if you have to guess, fill in *something*.

For 12th Grade:

- If you're not satisfied with your SAT or ACT score from the year before, sign up to take it again.

- Pick out the colleges that you're interested in attending. The ones you choose should have degrees that interest you. If they don't, and you're only planning on going there because your girlfriend or best friend is going there, then you'll have a less than successful college education.

- Find out all of the application requirements and deadlines for every college you choose. Most of the deadlines occur toward the middle of October through the end of November. Get yourself a calendar and write every single one of them down.

Sample Applications

Below is the 'Common Application' that you will find for most universities throughout the United States today. Some colleges still prefer to use their own format, though the Common Application has become more standard in recent years. You can fill the Common Application out and submit it online (preferred) or you can print it out and mail it per instructions based on the college or university you choose to apply to.

2012-13 FIRST-YEAR APPLICATION
For Spring 2013 or Fall 2013 Enrollment

APPLICANT

Legal Name _____
Last (family) name (Enter name exactly as it appears on official documents.)   First/Given   Middle (complete)   Jr., etc.

Preferred name, if not first name (only one) _____

Former last name(s) _____

Birth Date _____ ○ Female ○ Male
mm/dd/yyyy

US Social Security Number, if any _____
Required for US Citizens and Permanent Residents applying for financial aid via FAFSA

Preferred Telephone ○ Home ○ Cell   Home (___) _____
Area/Country/City Code

Cell (___) _____
Area/Country/City Code

E-mail Address [_____]

IM Address _____

Permanent home address _____
Number & Street   Apartment #

_____
City/town   Country or Parish   State/Province   Country   ZIP/Postal Code

If different from above, please give your current mailing address for all admission correspondence.   (from _____ to _____)
mm/dd/yyyy   *mm/dd/yyyy*

Current mailing address _____
Number & Street   Apartment #

_____
City/town   Country or Parish   State/Province   Country   ZIP/Postal Code

If your current mailing address is a boarding school, include name of school here: _____

FUTURE PLANS

Your answers to these questions will vary for different colleges. If the online system did not ask you to answer some of the questions you see in this section, this college chose not to ask that question of its applicants.

College _____

Deadline _____
mm/dd/yyyy

Entry Term: ○ Fall (Jul-Dec) ○ Spring (Jan-Jun)

Decision Plan: _____

Academic Interests _____

Career Interest _____

Do you intend to apply for need-based financial aid? ○ Yes ○ No
Do you intend to apply for merit-based scholarships? ○ Yes ○ No
Do you intend to be a full-time student? ○ Yes ○ No
Do you intend to enroll in a degree program your first year? ○ Yes ○ No
Do you intend to live in college housing?
What is the highest degree you intend to earn?

DEMOGRAPHICS

Citizenship Status _____

Non-US Citizenship _____

Birthplace _____
City/town   *State/Province*   *Country*

Years lived in the US? _____ Years lived outside the US? _____

Language Proficiency (Check all that apply.)
(Check: 1 (best) 2 (first) 3 (next) 4 (native or natural))
S   R   W   F   H
○ ○ ○ ○ ○
○ ○ ○ ○ ○
○ ○ ○ ○ ○

Optional The items with a gray background are optional. No information you provide will be used in a discriminatory manner.

Religious Preference _____

US Armed Services veteran status _____

1. Are you Hispanic/Latino?
○ Yes, Hispanic or Latino (including Spain) ○ No If yes, please describe your background.

2. Regardless of your answer to the prior question, please indicate how you identify yourself. (Check one or more and describe your background.)
○ American Indian or Alaska Native (including all Original Peoples of the Americas)
   Are you Enrolled? ○ Yes ○ No If yes, please enter Tribal Enrollment Number
○ Asian (including Indian subcontinent and Philippines)
○ Black or African American (including Africa and Caribbean)
○ Native Hawaiian or Other Pacific Islander (Original Peoples)
○ White (including Middle Eastern)

AP-1/2012-13

View the full common application, in PDF format, at:

https://www.commonapp.org/

Sample Application from a Public University (Western Connecticut State University):

Application for Admission — Please read all questions carefully and print (or type) neatly.

I am applying for: ○ Full-time status ○ Part-time status   Semester ○ Fall ○ Spring   Year: _____

Is this your first application to Western Connecticut State University?   ○ Yes ○ No
If no, what is the approximate date of previous application? _____

■ Legal Name

Legal name (last, first, middle initial)

Previous (maiden) name

Social security number (recommended)

Date of birth (MM/DD/YY)   Place of birth (city, state)

■ Contact Information

Primary e-mail address (Important: This e-mail address will be used as the primary communication medium regarding the status of your application.)

Street address

City, state & ZIP   Country, if outside U.S.A.

Length of time at current address

Previous address (if applicable)

Previous city, state & ZIP (if applicable)   Country, if outside U.S.A.

Home telephone (with area code)   Mobile telephone (with area code)   Work telephone (with area code)

Parent(s) name(s)

Parent(s) address, if different from above (include city, state and ZIP)

■ Citizenship & Personal Information

Gender: ○ Male ○ Female

Are you a veteran?   ○ Yes ○ No

Citizenship: ○ U.S. Citizen   ○ Non-citizen
If you are a non-citizen:
Do you hold an Alien Registration Receipt Card (green card)? ○ No ○ Yes (if yes, indicate alien no.: _____)
Please provide a photocopy of: ○ F-1 Student Visa   ○ F-2 Student Visa   ○ Other Visa Status

In order to meet State and Federal requirements, we are requesting that you voluntarily supply the following information. This data will not be used for discriminatory purposes and will not be considered in the evaluation of your application.

What is your ethnicity?   ○ Hispanic or Latino   ○ Neither Hispanic nor Latino

What is your race? (Mark all that may apply)
○ White   ○ Black or African-American   ○ Asian
○ American Indian or Alaska Native   ○ Native Hawaiian or Other Pacific Islander

Is English your native language?   ○ Yes ○ No

What is your religious preference? _____

■ Athletics

Are you interested in playing a varsity sport here?   ○ Yes ○ No
If yes, please select from the list below:

Men   Women
○ baseball   ○ basketball   ○ swimming & diving
○ basketball   ○ field hockey   ○ tennis
○ football   ○ lacrosse   ○ volleyball
○ lacrosse   ○ soccer
○ soccer   ○ softball
○ tennis

You can review the rest of this application, in PDF format, at:

http://www.wcsu.edu/admissions/application/wcsu_ugrad_application_1112.pdf

For private schools, which are not government subsidized, such as Stanford University, Harvard, and George Washington University, they also utilize the Common Application.

For community colleges, Butler County Community College in Pennsylvania uses the following application form:

Application for Admission

Please complete the following information as accurately as possible. This information is required for admission.

NAME : _____
             Last   First   Middle

PERMANENT LEGAL ADDRESS : _____

CITY : _____ STATE : _____ ZIP CODE : _____ COUNTY OF RESIDENCE : _____

HOME PHONE NUMBER : ( ) _____

CELL PHONE NUMBER : ( ) _____

SOCIAL SECURITY NUMBER : _____ - ____ - _____

Your Social Security number is required for financial aid eligibility, scholarships, veterans benefits, and IRS tax reporting purposes. To protect your privacy, it will not be used as your student identification number. You will be given a BC3 student ID number for identification.

GENDER: _____ DATE OF BIRTH : _____ / _____ / _____

In order to gather information required by state and federal agencies, we are requesting that you provide the following information. Your answer to these questions will in no way affect your admission status. Further, this information will be held confidential and used only for statistical purposes.

DO YOU CONSIDER YOURSELF TO BE HISPANIC / LATINO? _____ YES / NO
                                       Circle One

IN ADDITION, SELECT ONE OR MORE OF THE FOLLOWING RACIAL CATEGORIES TO DESCRIBE YOURSELF:

- [ ] AMERICAN INDIAN/ALASKAN NATIVE
- [ ] ASIAN
- [ ] BLACK/AFRICAN AMERICAN
- [ ] NATIVE HAWAIIAN/OTHER PACIFIC ISLANDER
- [ ] WHITE

PERSONAL E-MAIL ADDRESS : _____

Be sure to activate your MyBC3 e-mail account. Once accepted as a BC3 student, the College will communicate with you through your student e-mail address.

APPLICATION YEAR : _____ TERM : _____ 2-Fall / 3-Spring / 4-Summer
                                          Circle One

IF YOU SELECTED SUMMER, WILL YOU BE ENROLLED AT BC3 IN THE FALL? _____ YES / NO / NA
                                          Circle One

PROGRAM FOR WHICH YOU ARE APPLYING : _____ PROGRAM OF STUDY : _____
                               Enter Program Code From Page 4

COLLEGE EXPERIENCE: Select all that apply

- [ ] FIRST TIME AT ANY COLLEGE
- [ ] TRANSFER FROM ANOTHER COLLEGE TO BC3
- [ ] GUEST STUDENT VISITING FROM ANOTHER COLLEGE
- [ ] PREVIOUSLY ATTENDED BC3

EDUCATIONAL GOAL: _____ Associate / Basic coursework / Non-Degree Seeking / Certificate
                                          Circle One

You can view this application form, in PDF format, at:

http://www.bc3.edu/pdf/admissionapp.pdf

Sample Reference Letters

Reference letters are basically letters of recommendation from people that know you. This doesn't mean you should have your best friend write them, but rather choose a teacher or two, or if there is an adult with whom you've worked within the community who values your effort and dedication, these kinds of recommendations can go a long way.

Below are a couple of sample reference (recommendation) letters.

Attn: Julia M. Jones
Re: Katie Kingston

Dear Ms. Jones:

I am writing this reference at the request of Katie Kingston who is applying for Student Volunteer Program at St. Francis Hospital this summer.

I have known Katie for two years in my capacity as a teacher at Smithtown Middle School School. Katie took English and Spanish from me and earned superior grades in those classes. Based on Katie's grades, attendance and class participation, I'd rate Katie's academic performance in my class as superior.

Katie has a number of strengths to offer an employer. Katie is always interested in supporting others. For example, this year when we worked on our class community service project, Katie was helpful to me in collecting and organizing the food for the food pantry here in Smithtown.

In conclusion, I would highly recommend Katie Kingston. If her performance in my class is any indication of how she'd perform in your position, Katie will be a positive addition to your organization. If you should ever need any additional information you can feel free to contact me at 555-5555 or by email at email@email.com anytime.

Sincerely,

Susan Samuels
Teacher, Smithtown Middle School

(from http://jobsearch.about.com/od/referenceletters/a/sampleteachref2.htm)

A second sample recommendation letter:

To Whom It May Concern:

Carrie Youstis is an exceptional young lady. Most everyone knows of her intellectual acumen, lofty ambitions, dancing abilities, and kindness; indeed, she is a sort of legend in her small hometown of Southwest Plainsfield, NJ, but few know of the struggle Carrie endured during her middle years of high school. Carrie had a close friend, Kaya, whom she had met at summer camp. She and Kaya had grown very close during the first two years of high school.

During the middle of tenth grade, Carrie received news that Kaya was suffering from a rare degenerative disease. It was terminal, Carrie was told but did not cry. She did not even take a moment to worry about how this might affect her. She simply called me, her principal, and asked if she could miss a few days of school, explaining to me the grave situation. I told her that, of course, she may miss school, provided that she make up her work.

Then, before she hung up, Carrie asked me to pray on her friend's behalf, and said, " I can go on without Kaya -- I have many friends and I will mourn but I have a wonderful life. Kaya is suffering so much, though, and when it' s all over, that will be it for her. And she is her mother' s only child. How will she go on?" I was so impressed that Carrie was thinking about everyone affected except herself: Kaya, Kaya's mother, but not Carrie Youstis. Such maturity. Carrie knew she had a wonderful life, a belief in God, but she felt for others so profoundly.

Carrie visited Kaya often for several months, always bringing her cards and flowers and of course, good cheer. Kaya finally passed away that Spring, and Carrie made sure to visit the mother every week that following summer.

You will read of Carrie's grades and scores and sports abilities, of her awards and accolades; I wanted to relate this episode, as it characterizes what this remarkable young lady is really all about. As she graduates high school, I and all of Southwest Plainsfield are so sad to see her go, but realize that she is destined to effect great things far beyond the narrow confines of a small town in New Jersey.

Sincerely,

Esti Iturralde
Principal, North Southwest Plainsfield High School

(from: http://businessmajors.about.com/od/samplerecommendations/a/RecSample9.htm)

It is highly recommended that you not use 'To Whom It May Concern,' however. Instead, address the letter to the admissions committee or, better yet, find out the name of the admissions director at the university to which you're applying.

If you need more help understanding the application process, visit http://www.march2success.com/index.cfm.

1. What happens when you leave answers blank on a SAT exam?

2. Name one web site that can help you prepare for the ACT and SAT.

3. Name one thing you can do your Senior year to prepare for college admissions.

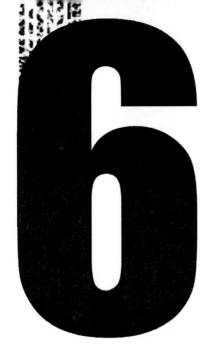

Aiming for the Right Schools

Sure, you may have the greatest ambition in the world and have discovered I.M. Pei and have decided that you, too, can become one of the most innovative architects in the world, but if you've skated by with B's and C's, don't set your sights on MIT or Cal-Tech.

There are thousands of colleges and universities around the country that you can choose from. Some of them are going to be intensely difficult to get into (i.e. Yale, Harvard, the aforementioned MIT) and others will give you a great opportunity to advance your education.

Be realistic in your approach to colleges. Look at their admission rates (you can find a wealth of this information by simply searching online), the size of the student body, the programs and degree choices that they offer, and what they're usual requirements are as far as grades, SAT/ACT scores, and more.

If you are not realistic in your goals and expectations, you could find yourself banking on a few choice schools and not be accepted to any of them. This will set you back and you'll have to start the process all over again. When that happens, the opportunity to give up increases. Don't put yourself in that position.

Focus on Your Interests

What strikes your interest and sparks passion in your life is something that can carry you through the tough days of studying, the challenging work of writing a thesis paper for your final grade, and pulling an 'all nighter' studying for your last exam of your college education.

Each school will generally have a few specialty programs (for example, engineering would be a program, as would psychology or nursing) that they place a greater emphasis on than others. This doesn't mean any other program at these schools are secondary or not worth your time, but each school is competing with hundreds of others for students and have to specialize.

So, for example, you may be interested in nursing. In that case, you'll want to apply to those colleges that have invested in a solid nursing program.

Look at the graduation rate of those schools. Find out how many students who start certain programs finish them and also what percentage of graduates find jobs within their chosen field. All of this information can be obtained through the college admissions department.

What Are the School's Requirements?

Overall, most colleges throughout the country require an official high school transcript, an application (that can usually be obtained through the school's website), one or two reference letters, and an essay that will be written by the applying student (you).

However, there might be a number of other requirements as well, so it's important that you know what they expect before you begin the application process.

Each school will have an application fee. Determine how much these are and make sure that you will have enough money to apply to the colleges you choose. Some will provide waivers, depending on your family's economic resources and availability.

I know we mentioned this already, but make sure you know *all* of the school's deadlines.

A school may require your application by October 15th, for example. The essay may not be due until November 30th, though. Write everything down and do *not* miss a deadline. This isn't like turning in your homework assignment late and still earning a grade for it. If you submit any part of your application late, you'll be diverted to the following semester or the next year's decision process.

Establish an Order of Preference

You should choose at least 5 colleges to apply to. Have one 'stretch' school. This will be a school that you consider an elite school, one for which your grades might fall below their generally accepted levels. It should be a school that would provide you with the best opportunity for success within the field of interest you currently possess.

Next, choose two 'safe' schools. These will be schools that you are quite confident that you will be accepted to. Their expectations for grades won't be as high as your 'stretch' school, and they might not have the best program, but they can provide you with a solid education and foundation for the rest of your life.

Finally, choose at least two 'preferred' schools. These will be schools that you would prefer to attend, but you aren't sure that you'll be accepted into them. Your preferred schools will be the kind that you would choose if you were accepted to all the schools you applied to aside from your stretch school.

There are a vast array of resources available online that can help you launch your career even before you start college. The Emma Bowen Foundation, for example, helps students interested in a career within the media get moving in that direction. Find out more by visiting the website at: http://www.emmabowenfoundation.org.

What about Financial Assistance?

You might be thinking, "This is all great, but I can't afford to go to college. My family doesn't earn enough money to pay for me to go."

There are a number of public and private financial assistance packages that almost anyone can take advantage of. Harvard, for example, ensures that everyone who is accepted can attend. If your family's financial resources can't afford it, they would pay for all of your tuition, room and board, and books. MIT is similar and there are hundreds of schools across the country that provide similar assistance. Though most wouldn't be able to pay for everything, they can certainly help out.

You could take out a student loan through FAFSA (Federal government-backed, low interest loans), earn grants or scholarships, and look at working part time at the college you attend.

Once you've finished applying, it's time to look into the type of financial assistance you would receive.

If you have a limited financial ability to pay, keep in mind that in-state public universities will charge less for tuition and room and board than you would pay if you attended a public college out of state. In other words, if you can't afford much, focus on in-state public colleges. For now.

FAFSA provides opportunities to obtain low interest, government-backed loans. Visit http://www.fafsa.ed.gov to learn more. You can also find more information about FAFSA in Chapter 9 and the Resources section.

Long Distance or Close to Home?

Right now, the idea of living far away from home, having that incredible sense of independence, is alluring. If you could get into a school that is across the country, you might just jump at that opportunity right now, wouldn't you?

However, you want to make this kind of decision with a clear mind.

Are you close to your family? What about friends? If you travel several hundred of even thousands of miles away from home, it will cost more to get back for visits. With the price of gas today and airfare climbing through the roof, you need to make sure that if you go to a school that's a good distance away you're going to be comfortable and happy.

You can often find the same level of independence and excitement by attending a school that's less than an hour's drive from home as well. This can provide you with the opportunity to pop back home for a weekend visit every now and then, see your friends, and even give your friends an opportunity to come out and visit you on campus.

When considering a college, distance is important, so take the time to make a reasonable decision about it.

Chapter 6 Get In Gear Questions

1. Most colleges and universities require what for the application process?

2. How many colleges should you apply to?

3. What should all students apply for that may allow them to be eligible for low interest loans and/or grants?

The Essay

Okay, so you can't stand writing. You're not alone. But the college application essay could very well be the most important aspect of the entire process.

It could be the most important thing you write during your entire life.

Okay, okay, we're exaggerating a little bit here, but we're trying to impress upon you the importance of the essay.

Almost every college requires you to write one. Each college will have their own topic for you to write about (and it's not going to be 'What I Did on My Summer Vacation'). And it's important for *you* to write it.

Spend two minutes on the Internet and you'll be able to find about a hundred websites that provide writing services. You could probably find someone to write an essay for you for less than $20. But that won't help you get into the college of your choice and here's why: your essay is the chance for you to *show* the admissions board the passion you have in life, your *desire* to excel and achieve your goals, and let them see a side of you that is beyond your grades, beyond your SAT or ACT score, and that is *more* than the activities you partake in.

So take the challenge on yourself and write your essay. By yourself.

Now, what to write about.

What to Write About

Most college essays questions will have to do with something you've done in your life, some event that has transformed you, or some specific experience that you find revolutionary (something that could have changed your life, moved you in a specific direction).

They could ask about current events of social issues. They might ask about personal achievements. They might want to know about your future goals or what influences you've had in your life. They might even ask about a book or person that has influenced you.

Many colleges will offer a choice between two topics, so you're bound to find something to write about that will show them that you're their kind of student and impress upon them that you truly care about getting a college education and degree.

Below are a few sample questions that you *might* see for the application essay:

- Describe a time when you demonstrated leadership, whether in school or within your community.
- What is your opinion about the current political landscape in this country?

- What book have you read that impacted your life? Explain.

- What are your short-term goals? What are your long-term goals?

- How has your upbringing (where you live and your family) affected the way you see the world?

- Tell us about one person who has shaped or altered your life in a way that has been positive.

- What do you want to get out of your college education?

- Describe your most meaningful achievement to date and explain why you believe this to be the case.

- Describe a unique attribute or special achievement that separates you from those around you.

As you can see, there are a host of topics that you can choose to write about, but you want to make sure that the question your school asks is answered with your essay. This could mean that you'll have to write more than one essay.

Now, as far as writing that essay …

Why You Need to Write It

You know yourself best. Sure, you might not like to write or maybe you don't think that you have the skills to create a powerful and inspiring essay, but you'll likely surprise yourself.

In truth, college admissions committee members often note how they can tell immediately whether the person whose grades and activities are listed before them actually wrote the essay.

You have a specific and unique 'voice' and tone about your personality and that will come through in your writing. Also, if you generally earned 'C' grades in English classes and your teacher considered your writing efforts to be satisfactory, then delivering polished and profound prose in your essay is going to shine like a beacon, telling the college, 'This student didn't write his (or her) essay!'

Another reason why it's important for you to write your own essay has to do with *passion*.

We've used this word on several occasions already, and we'll keep using it.

Why?

Because *passion* is important. Not only in school and ultimately work, but in all aspects of life. If you don't have passion, you'll have a job. If you don't have passion, you won't excel. If you don't have passion, you'll end up in listless relationships with friends who don't fulfill your life.

Passion is what drives the most successful people in life. When I talk about 'successful' people, I'm not talking about Bill Gates or Barack Obama, though they are two great examples of successful individuals. I'm talking about people from your own neighborhoods, people who may not have a lot of money but who do great things in their community, for their family, or for their job.

If you truly desire a college education, the essay is where you can convince them that you're ready to take charge, to contribute, to be a student who will be an *asset* to their campus.

You will never convey that in an essay if you have someone else write it.

Never.

Most college essays are only 300 to 500 words. They may be two parts. It's an afternoon, at most, to write the first draft.

Take the time to write it yourself.

The Writing Process, in Brief

I could write an entire book on writing a college entrance essay, but there are plenty of them already on the market. Pick up one or two and read through them.

However, the writing process is relatively straightforward. It follows as:

1. *Write the first draft.* When it comes to the first draft, just write. Choose your topic, think about what you'll discuss in the essay, and then just write. Don't worry about grammar or spelling. Don't worry about sentence structure or how it may sound. Just write. Write until you're done. If you write 1,000 words or more, that's fine. Just write.

2. *Set it aside.* Leave it alone for a few days once you finish the first draft. This is the time to forget about what you wrote and let your mind refresh.

3. *Read your first draft.* After a few days, go back over what you wrote and read it. Parts of it should sound familiar while other parts will leave you scratching your head, thinking, 'I wrote that?' Just read it. Don't make any notes. Just read.

4. *Edit.* Once you've read it through, go back and re-read it again, right away. This time, do so with a red or blue pen (if you wrote it in black or typed it on your computer). Make notes and comments about the grammar or structure. Check for spelling. If you've written more than the word count allows, cut out parts that don't add to your story. It can be tough, but sometimes you just have to take out things you like the most.

5. *Polish.* Once you've expanded or condensed your essay to fit within the desired word count, it's time to polish it. If you're not good with grammar, ask your English teacher to go over it *with you.* Don't ask him or her to edit it for you; you won't learn and it will suddenly become an essay that is no longer truly yours. Your teacher may tell you to rewrite certain sentences, but you also want to maintain your unique 'voice' and style. Use your discretion at this point.

6. *Have 5 people read it.* Choose 5 people to read your essay and give their impressions about it. Family, friends, the guy at the corner deli … whoever. Ask them to give their *honest* impressions about it. Then listen. You might not like what they say, but if the

majority of them tell you the same thing–that something's not ringing true or doesn't read well–then you may want to rework that part of your essay.

That's it.

Now, get to writing.

Chapter 7 Get In Gear Questions

1. What is one of the most important aspects of the college application process?

2. What do most college essay questions have to do with?

3. Why is passion important?

The Visit

You want to be comfortable at the college you attend, so it's important that you visit as many as you can.

There's a life and vibrancy within many college campuses that you simply won't get the feel for unless you physically walk the campus, speak to some of the students, and ask *important* questions.

Unfortunately, most high school students simply sleepwalk through the visit. They boys want to know where the girls' dorms are, where the pool hall is, and what the parties are like. Girls want to know about sororities, boys' dorms, and maybe where the closest mall is.

But these aren't important, not in the grand scheme of things. Think about what will be important to you when you settle in, once classes start, and when you're looking at improving your grades.

Where is the library? If you end up in a dorm that's a far distance from the library, you're less apt to use it for studying. If it's not close to where you might live, does the residence hall have a study room? How secure are the residence halls? Would people have to be checked in before accessing the main part of the building?

Here are some tips to keep in mind when it comes to visiting the college for the first time:

1. *Go to the student union.* There are usually a great deal of things that you'll find in most student unions. This is where you might find food, a bookstore, study rooms, and other resources that you will likely find useful during your time here.

2. *Check out the cafeteria.* You won't know what the food is going to be like or how convenient the cafeteria is by looking at a few pictures in a flyer or brochure. Be certain to check them out on your visit. Most schools will allow you the opportunity to eat in one of the cafeterias while you're there for your visit.

3. *Look at the commons rooms.* Almost every dorm will have commons rooms. This is where you will find couches and recliners or other chairs and perhaps a television set. Students enjoy hanging out here from time to time, studying, or just stretching their legs outside of the confines of their actual dorm room. Think of a commons room as a living room or den in a house; it's available to everyone.

4. *Speak to an R.A.* A resident advisor is generally a person who keeps order among the dorms. Each hall generally has an R.A. and it's a good idea to meet one, ask questions, and get a better feel for what your life on campus will be like.

5. *Visit some of the freshman classrooms.* Most colleges don't have specific classrooms for different years, but many of the freshman classes will be held in

larger settings, as more students take these first year classes. When you visit a few classrooms, you will get a sense about how different things are between college and high school.

Ask Questions

When you plan to visit a college, prepare a number of questions. Make sure that they pertain to college living and studying. Avoid trying to be funny.

You may be the funniest kid in your school and get every student chuckling at your jokes and comments, but you'll more often find a mute response when you act that way on a college campus.

Below are a few questions that are a good start for you to think about:

1. *What does this college look for in a student?*
2. *How much will it cost me to attend school here?*
3. *What is the graduation rate?*
4. *Are there other students like me? Or will I feel like an outcast?*
5. *Do they have a program that I'll be interested in?*

By preparing the questions that you should ask ahead of time, you will have more than enough information to make the right decision about which school you choose to attend.

Chapter 8 Get In Gear Questions

1. What is something you should prepare when planning a college visit?

2. What is an RA?

3. What are 3 possible questions to think of for your college visit?

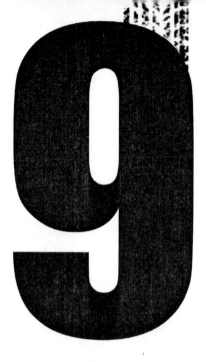

Affordability

One of the most common reasons that students say they won't go to college is because they don't think they can afford it.

The reality is that with all of the available scholarships, grants, and student loans that are available, no matter what your family's financial situation, or your own, there's no reason why you can't attend school.

The trick is to find out where the money is.

Show me the money! was a line from the movie *Jerry Maguire* with Cuba Gooding Jr. and Tom Cruise.

Find out what kind of scholarships or financial assistance the school offers. You can find out most of this information online by visiting the college's website, or calling and speaking to someone from financial aid services at the school.

Your high school guidance counselor will also be able to assist you in finding the information that you need.

Scholarships

Even if you don't think that you could possibly apply for any scholarships (maybe your grades aren't exceptional or you never took part in sports), there is a great deal of money available for college-bound students who have a sincere desire to attend and excel in college.

You will have to keep in mind that you would have to apply for about 75 scholarships to earn one. That may seem like an enormous amount of work, but it's really not all that bad.

However, think of it this way: if college is really that important to you, then wouldn't it stand to reason that you'd be willing to spend a fair amount of time on finding a way to pay for it?

And one positive aspect about scholarships is that they are not loans. You don't have to pay them back.

A scholarship is basically a grant, a gift of money from one organization or another that is designed to help alleviate the financial pressures that young college students endure while they seek to further their education.

When you know that you won't have to pay back scholarship money, you'll be thinking, 'What's the catch?'

The catch is that you have to maintain a specific GPA, usually at least above a 2.5, which would be determined by the organization that funds the scholarship. So, if you're truly sincere about wanting an education, then there should be no reason why you couldn't maintain a solid 2.5 (about a B) grade point average during your time in college.

Find a list of scholarships through http://www.scholarships.com and http://www.superscholar.org/scholarships/25-popular-college-scholarships/) or through Hispanic Scholarship Fund (http://www.latinocollegedollars.org) and the NAACP (www.naacp.org/youth/scholarships). These are just a few, but there are more scholarship resources to research, including plenty of companies and corporations that offer scholarships.

FAFSA

The federal government offers a number of loans that you could apply for. These loans are provided on a first come, first served basis, and the only determination is financial need.

If you can prove that you can't afford to attend school without a student loan, then you will likely qualify for it.

What is nice about a FAFSA student loan is that the interest doesn't begin accruing until you graduate and no payments are required until a few months after you have earned your diploma.

What you want to think about when it comes to college's affordability is that you can always live at home and go to a college that is close by, at least for the first couple of years while you figure out what you truly want to do with your life.

If you don't live on campus, taking a couple of classes per semester, it will cost you less than a monthly car payment would for a new car.

Once you realize that college is more affordable than you might have thought, it should inspire you to want to attend college even more. Does it?

I thought so. Get more information or to begin the application process, visit FAFSA's website: http://www.fafsa.ed.gov. You will need your parent's support with the application if you're not yet 18 years of age.

Chapter 9 Get In Gear Questions

1. What is one of the most common reasons students state for not being able to attend college?

2. How many scholarships should every student apply for?

3. Federal government loans are provided based upon what need?

Decision Time

Well, you've done all of the hard work, applied to a variety of colleges, and now the mail starts to arrive.

Each trip to the mailbox leaves you with a little anxiousness. You're nervous and excited at the same time.

You already know which schools are on your preferred list and which ones are your 'safe' schools.

But you're like anyone else in this world … until you know for sure, until you have that acceptance letter (or package) in your hands, then you're going to have some doubts.

You should already have visited the schools and done your homework about what they provide to you. If you haven't, or you need to refresh, now is the time. As you get an acceptance letter, write down all of the positives that the school provides for you and your educational needs.

If you receive a rejection letter, toss it out. There's no reason to focus on the rejections.

We all get them in life. Honestly, if you ask most people, even the most successful ones, you'll learn that they received many rejection letters through the years. They aren't a reflection on the person that you are.

Besides, if you truly applied to schools that were considered a 'stretch' for you, then those shouldn't come as a surprise.

Don't let them discourage you.

Now, make your list of the positive attributes that the school that accepted you offers. On a second list, provide all the negative points (too far, too big, more expensive, etc).

Once you have your list, you'll be able to look at and compare all of the schools that accepted you with an unbiased perspective.

However, you're going to have one in particular that calls to you more. One school will be on your mind more than others and it is this school that will be tough to turn down.

Yes, your instincts matter. But don't be driven by your desires for distance from family, the allure of a 'party' school, or the belief that one school will change your life.

You will change your life. Nothing else.

If you go off to college with the mindset that just doing that act alone is going to alter your life, then you're going to be sorely disappointed with the results.

College is your launching pad to a better life. It is the opportunity to make a fresh start and begin pursuing all that you hope to achieve in life.

So, when you get that first acceptance letter, celebrate. Dance. Tell your family, tell your friends.

Bring it to school and show the teachers who matter to you.

Enjoy the moment, then begin the process of sorting through all of the information you've acquired through the months of researching and applying to these schools.

Make sure you know when the deadline is for making a decision that each school determines for itself.

The last thing you want is to miss the deadline of your chosen school, fail to let them know you're coming in the fall, and lose your place to someone else.

Now, let's see what amazing things you'll accomplish in the rest of your life.

Oh, and congratulations.

1. What should you be doing as your receive your acceptance letters?

2. The college you select to attend should NOT be driven by what factor?

3. What is college a launching pad for?

Know How 2 Go

It's never too early to prepare for college. Knowhow2go.com provides great resources and information so that you can stay ahead of the game when it comes to getting ready to apply for, and be accepted to, the college of your choice. http://www.knowhow2go.com/

Number 2

When you understand the importance of scoring well on the SAT or ACT exams, Number2.com provides assistance in helping you prepare and get the score that you deserve. https://www.number2.com/

Do Something

Want to become involved in a worthy cause? It will not only make you feel great, it will be impressive on that college application. Dosomething.org is a great place to start. http://www.dosomething.org/

Career One Stop

Perhaps you need a job right now, before thinking about college. Careeronestop.org can provide the necessary tools to help you land the job that fits your needs and schedule. http://www.careeronestop.org/

Emma Bowen Foundation

If you have an interest in a possible career within the media, the Emma Bowen Foundation can be a solid stepping stone. http://emmabowenfoundation.org

College Week Live

Get the inside track on the latest news and information from a number of colleges around the country with Collegeweeklive.com. http://www.collegeweeklive.com/

March 2 Success

Understanding the college application process and learning how to prepare for the SAT or ACT tests are important and March2Success.com can help. https://www.march2success.com/index.cfm

FAFSA

The Federal Government provides assistance and government backed, low interest loans for students. Find out more and how to apply at:

http://www.fafsa.ed.gov/

Hispanic Scholarship Fund

The Hispanic Scholarship Fund provides assistance to those minorities who may not otherwise be able to afford to attend college.

http://www.hsf.net/

Hispanic Scholarship Fund Search Tool

This helps you find a number of scholarships that are available to Latinos to help pay for college. It also has scholarships for undocumented students. This resource isn't providing a scholarship, but it will find some that you can apply for.

http://www.latinocollegedollars.org/

UNCF

UNCF is the nation's largest and most effective minority education organization. If you are a student attending a UNCF-member college or university, it is highly recommended that you also complete the UNCF general scholarship application and discover which of their scholarship programs you qualify for:

https://scholarships.uncf.org/

Scholarships

Find a number of scholarships that you can apply for (you'll likely discover that there are many wonderful possibilities that you qualify for):

http://www.scholarships.com/

http://www.superscholar.org/scholarships/25-popular-college-scholarships/